Seasonings

by

Cora E. Cypser

Published by

KIM PATHWAYS

Page Maker Sketches by Cora E. Cypser

Printed in U.S.
by BookMasters
Ashland, Ohio

Inquiries regarding requests to print all or part of *Seasonings* should be addressed to KIM PATHWAYS.

To order directly from the publisher add $1.50 to the price for the first copy and $.50 for each additional copy. Send check or money order to KIM PATHWAYS.

Opinions expressed in this book are not necessarily the views of the publisher.

For more information:

KIM PATHWAYS
101 Young Road
Katonah, NY 10536

Contents

iii

Dedicated to
all those who are attuned
to the changing of the seasons

Communication

Our lives touch for a moment
with this poetry!
Imagine--
for a bit of spinning earth
my spirit reaches out
and lays a claim on yours
with a layer of inky print
upon a page.

What can words do
frail, structured letters
marching in a line
drawn from an eager soul?

I wish
that in each poem
I have written
there were words
that could give peace
and healthiness
and understanding
as some with skill
sketch out a flower
or craft a scene.

Would that I
could write love.

I wish
that as our spirits touch
you would receive
great gifts
that only God can give
that make the human
a true child of God.

Ode to Time

You are strong.
I have felt your knotted arm
even when I thought
you were only a small boy
flexing his muscles.
Now I roll with the punches.

You are lovely.
Every time you turn
gracefully by me
you reveal some new beauty
so that I forget
you take as well as give.

You are my friend
holder of my mortgage on life
who has loaned me days
that may be transformed to service
which in turn may be traded for love.

Should I fear you
as I feel your loving fingers
running through my hag-gray hair?

The Season of Winter

Hiddenbrooke at The Foot of Mount Beacon

The forest is not silent.
God is not silent.
I heard a mountainside make music
through a film of frozen crystal
a unity of trees singing together.

You must go alone
to the edge of the woods and listen
for the sound of treetops praying
(though they stand
like motionless dead sticks).
There you will hear
like you were on the edge of eternity
a universal voice rising
from the multitude of winter trees.

The forest is not silent
and God is not silent.
There is a holy spirit buzzing
like bees drunk on locust trees in June
that rises from parched throats
which appear January frozen in our age
a universal voice that rises
from this community
of seemingly dead trees.

Hollowness

There is a gray-white hollow in the day
and God is filling it with snow
dear God, doing what is needed
filling the empty
cheering the bleak.

My heart reaches out to the day
and it, too, feels its hollowness
stretching out to meet
the gray-white emptiness.
Dear God, fill the empty!
God, cheer the bleak.

Who Sees The Half-moon?

The half-moon comes up at noon
but who sees it?
The brightness of the sun
confuses our eyes.

So in our country
the visibility of detente policies
almost makes oblivion
of peace negotiations.

So in our church
the formidableness of the hierarchy
blinds us to the equalizing love
that is necessary
among all human beings.

For Valentine's Day

Think it not strange, oh, Beloved
that we should be in love with God
(for God is all lovely)
my soul and your soul
in love
with the Soul that made the universe!

What kind of love is this
where one loves so much
that one is made over
into that which one loves?

I become like you.
You become like me.

We become like God.

Let us love God, then, greatly
as we gladly run to rendezvous.
Then if we keep the course
and reach the glorious goal
we shall find we are like God.

Lord, help us to keep our course.
Help us to reach that goal.

*Help us to **be** like you.*

Loneliness

I am loneliness.
I come to you
after the last sunbeam
on winter days.
I haunt you
through the shadows of your life.

I trail you along the roads
that are dark and wind beaten.

I am the devil of loneliness.
I come to torment you
on rainy nights and bleak days.
I am all the things you look back on
with longing.
I am all the things
you would like to have happen now
that won't happen.

I am a God you cannot believe in.
I am a lover who does not love.
I am work too hard to be done alone
that must be done
alone.

I am the devil of loneliness.
I come to you
in the great city
and I walk the streets with you
while you go up and down
up and down
searching for a friendly face
searching for a familiar heart.

Seasonings

I stalk beside you laughing
and casting futile and fragile memories
into your mind.
I chuckle wildly to myself
while you walk up and down
up and down
knowing you will never find
that which you seek.

I am loneliness.
I am the woman no man loves.
I am a broken violin.

I am a soldier wounded in battle.
I am a wild wind-swept song.

I haunt you
through the shadows of your life.

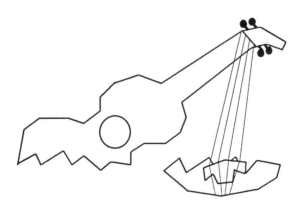

Hawk Thoughts

I reach out to the black hawk
sailing over the lake
and I feel that I can almost hold him
in my hand, that his being
is a part of my being.
But, no, I cannot confine him.
He is made to be free
in his place of melting ice
and cold February wind.

Does God feel like that about us--
spirits made of God's Spirit?
God does not confine us.
God lets us fly free.

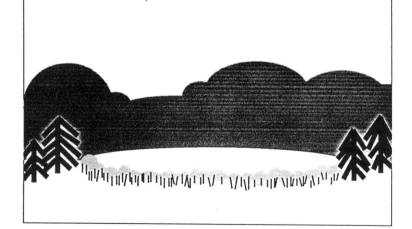

8

The Season of Spring

The Fir Tree

Like to a fir tree greening in the spring
I am as one
turning a fresher and more radiant look
to the warmer sun.

I stand with a new spirit, so it seems
straighter in my place
waking, and shaking off cold winter's dreams
seeking my master's face.

So what have I to do with storms
or winds that race
or with unnourishing sod?
I shall stand straighter
firmer, taller in my place
feeling the love of God.

Take A Springtime Road

A springtime road is a road that shines
in the morning sun.
A springtime road is a road to take
as the day's begun
but one must go with a springtime heart
and morning eyes
to tread a path suffused
with a gold sunrise.

Wall Song

Under the sun filled sky
a gray stone wall
ran up a green hill
in an aimless way
with rustling ivy
twisting on it all.
It was a perfect spot--
a perfect day.
There I sat
and my panting old dog lay.

We pantheists breathed deep
the mossy smell
that old walls have
and kept our eyes
upon a lazy snake
who'd thought to dwell
by this warm wall
under the sparkling skies
so he'd not slither near us
and surprise.

Each springtime journey
has its space
of guarded resting on a wall.
We must be cognizant
of snakes and possibilities
of fall.

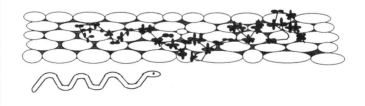

The Resurrection Robin

Yesterday it was cold and windy
and bleak and dreary.
Suddenly this morning I heard
the robin's cheery-cheery-cheery.
I watched him high in my oak tree
and thought how wonderful it was that he
should know inside his little head
that it was about time he said
a song of bird joy in my yard.

From years of springs I knew that now
the brown grass would turn green
and the forsythia would start to preen
herself, and I knew, too
that someday God would make things new
and that then we would certainly arise
to be with God in Paradise.
Spring comes to you
and comes to me
and likewise comes to us, eternity.
We cannot stop the robin from singing.

Renewal

God will create all things anew.
Lord, let me be near you then
to see you take the crooked
we have made, and to watch you
make it straight.

What a great day!
When all the good we pray
overcomes the bad we do
and your love turns us all to miracles!

Spring of The Cosmos

This is the day of the red bud maple.
The dust devils climb up spiral stairways
before laughing away in the wind.

The clouds say soft, hazy things
about an April shower tomorrow.
God speaks in the heart
that winter is never forever
though the worlds and the stars
freeze into oblivion.

Why There Are Black Holes in The Sky

I am the light, and you may call me Ray.
God made me on the first creative day.
My quivering photons all around you prance.
Hold fast onto my hand. See how I dance!

Through entities of liquid, gas, and space
in a mad pell-mell careless-seeming race
I rush to nowhere and return to fly
back to the infinite reaches of the sky.

I bend, my friend, when passing by the sun
bowing polite to his attractive mass
and if there were a star, a big dense one
that even my fast flight could not get past
then to its massive bosom I would fall
ignobly fast, and not be here at all.

Where would you be, without me?

Ode To God

They said we should write odes in praise
of those we love, or things we love
or lands we love, or ideas we love.

I said that I would praise the heavens
for they are wide
but you are wider than the heavens.

I said that I would praise time
for it is the leveler of all I see around
but you are timeless.

I said that I would praise spring
but when I considered its beauty
I thought of who made spring.

I said that I would praise love
but love as I knew it decayed, vanished
leaving only you standing there.

So I will sing to you, loving God
because you have tumbled the time-bound stars
across the spring-night heavens.

The Dancer

Spring
has turned the willow tree
into a Chinese dancer
whose golden sleeves
cover her lithe brown arms.

Indian Hymn

Our eager earth again sees springtime sweet.
The music of a thousand rivulets rings
for the Great Spirit will make things complete.

Whispers have come to fields of early wheat.
There are soft buzzing bugs and rustling wings.
Our eager earth again sees springtime sweet.

The brave bent with despair, near to defeat
has new hope stirring now, a heart that sings
for the Great Spirit will make things complete.

Leaves bud on boughs, laughing through frozen sleet.
Bulbs thrust up stalks through mulchy coverings.
Our eager earth again sees springtime sweet.

Some golden time our Indian souls will meet
in Happy Hunting Grounds as forest kings
for the Great Spirit will make things complete.

The end of winter brings on running feet
the joyful promise to renew all things.
Our eager earth again sees springtime sweet
for the Great Spirit will make things complete.

Trinity

I Am
the gardener
and the garden
and the tool
the gardener
uses.

As The Earth Approaches Omega

Things are so busy
bursting and blooming
thrusting and thrashing
bustle of blackbirds
tumult of tulips.

The earth seems an apex
of alert aliveness
amorphous with growth
ferine with fertility.

Are we near the great sound
of the triumphant trumpet
where man makes the choice
of God or explosion?

My Dandelion Bouquet

God, I shall pluck the days
as children gather dandelions
wildly, riotously
and offer them to you
with the same gay abandon
with the same assurance
that the common weed is lovely
as these children offer dandelions to me.

Will you accept these garish flowers, my days?
They may close up and look quite hideous
like this deceitful gold bouquet
but like the children
it is all I have to offer.

A New Generation

I come here among the fir trees to escape them
the green shoots, the wild new spring shoots
growing loudly
prodding up the earth ear-splittingly.

Faith is a dancer and claps her hands.
She does not know
the moon comes full each month.
She has never seen it before.
She says, "What is life?"

Hope is a drummer.
He splatters the sky with splinters.
He has led rats and mice
over the hill laughingly.
Hope says, "What is death?"

Charity strums the guitar.
She sings, "What is evil?"
The moon breathes back echoes.

I run away from their bombilation.
My ears cannot stand the fracas
the wild noise of spring green.
It's quiet here among the fir trees
who are too polite
to put forth queries I can't answer.

God's Music

The Mighty Hand pulled dust strands from a star
and made for us a world with all its rhythms
placing on it a syncopation full
of slithering bellies, shimmering fins
galloping hooves, and even agile minds
to romp across the swelling symphony.

"Music is good, but it needs song," God mused.
Therewith, the Mighty Voice sent forth the Word.

Oh, all ears listen! Learn the Word God sent!
Oh, all lips sing; put God's Word to God's music!

Open Your Eyes and See Rebirth

Look at the maples pendulous with bud
pregnant and red against a sapphire sky
the willows waving golden wands like rays
drawn from a sun in some child's picture
the haze leaning blue gray on the Catskills
gentle hills where we can climb
to rest under the stars
the silver beige of blades blown in the field
and over and surrounding all, the wind
the warm spring wind, the Holy Spirit wind
changing earth, making earth warm
giving earth a new heart.

Bless the whole world, Lord
because as all the trees are taught
to bud in spring
so all persons are taught
to desire you.

Becoming

The whole air is pulsing with God.
The rocks breathe God.
Something in matter, in flesh
aches to be spirit
longs to unite with glory
with eternity
with ultimate reality.

So look at us
striving to become
we know not what.

We disgorge all our energy
giving our innermost selves
to be a willing part
of that which formed us.

Knowledge Increases Mercy

*so let us **know***
until our very hearts
explode in love.

Passiontide

The Stations of The Cross

Station III
Falling

We walked with him
and childlike
mimed
his lilting step.
We paused by sun-filled doors
to laugh and heal.
We praised
through fields of wheat
feasted on grass green hills
burgeoned with a Palm Sunday
type of bliss.
But now it's turned to this!--

We see a worn and weary man
listing with loathsome load
battered, bruising his knees
along a jeering, jarring road
feet cloddishly plodding.

Do we trudge after?

We care not
to match this stride.
We run away
and hide.

The Stations of The Cross

Station V
Simon of Cyrene

*Black man confined
behind bars made of mistrust
and misunderstanding
you talk to me
white woman
of God Christ
and we forget
our skin shades
and our sexes
in the wonder
of healing wisdom.*

*Son of Cyrene's Simon
on your black back bear
the indiscriminate indignities
of creed and color
for the love
of antagonist nations
for our whole writhing world
and particularly for him
who was
Jew Jesus
son of the synagogue
who underwrote
all our un-love.*

The Stations of The Cross

Station VI
Veronica

See
the true image
on my veil!

I wiped
that sweaty, bloody brow
and found his spirit
stamped on mine
and now I know
that what I am
must properly retrace
the loving look
upon that faltering face.

I must not fail
to show
his wisdom
peace
in grave detail
in spite of how
my own humanity
my petty personal faults
my overburdening care
get in the way.

When someone looks at me
I must be sure
they see Christ there.

The Stations of The Cross

Station VIII
Weeping Women

Line up
on the pathway
weak women!
Watch
what your brothers do!
Watch
mankind rampage!
In their uncertainty
and insecurity
they heap a pile
of wounds and weapons.
They can't trust God
so pity them.

Weeping women
nursing babies
clutching toddlers
by the hand
contortedly
pity your sons
growing to blindness
hardness.
How can you get God closer
so they will see him
and remember?

What can you do
world's women
but prepare spices
for the burial?

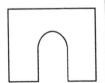

The Stations of The Cross

Station X
Stripping

It seems obscene
to dirty that nice robe
with dripping blood
so peel him bare!
Leave him just tortured flesh
feeling there!

Serve up a recipe
of nailing and thorning.
Spread on one human hulk.
Let connoisseurs taste it
in a carpeted church
on a later-day morning.

Station XII
Dying

He shouts out, "My God, why?"
just like I cry
in doubt, despair
as we smother on our crosses
viewing each other
across two thousand years
of joys and losses.
We both proclaim our pain
but he sees through it
to a future vindication
that escapes me.
If I walked in his ways
saw through his eyes
perhaps I, too, could
talk of paradise.

The Stations of The Cross

Station XII
The Sacrifice

"This is my body!"
words easy enough
for you to say
white robed priest
go-between of God and man.

Out on the hillside
even Brother Son
hid his face
behind obscuring fingers
and would not look
on how the human species
treats its own.

"This is my blood!"
Priest, do you hear
the gasping
feel the stickiness
the sweat, the lack of sleep
the infinite frustration
that this crude pitcher of a self
pours out in puddles
near your feet?

How does this mass
of convulsed flesh
add up
with gentle God's requirements
of wanting only mercy
justice
and a humble walking
with God's self?

Holy Spirit on Good Friday

Spirit, like fire
come!
Come back to Jesus, the Son
who hangs on the cross
crying
questioning
forsaken
dying.

Spirit, sear us
gently.
We are so fragile-human.
We watch flames
lick greedy tongues on logs
leaving them charcoal lumps.

We watch
fire's thirst to destroy
its yen to obliterate.
We wonder what demons
desires
heats
energies
are being released.

Come, Spirit, like fire
and tell us what is left
besides charcoal
and crosses
and corpses.

Asylum in Spring

The blossoms burst
against a sapphire sky
but it is always
winter of the heart here
and these, God's smallest ones
are kept apart here
and do not know or care
or see or try--
the tall men with strong voices
saying naught
the silent ones
who seem to hear no tone
to feel no touch
so hopelessly alone
the violent ones.

What can we do but aught--
servers who serve
doctors who strive to cure
seeking where knowledge
is too weak to go?
Where is the Christ
to cast their devils out
into the swine
and they stand
new and pure?

Oh, God
when will these gates of hell break wide
letting the springtime in on every side?

Comment on The Sacredness of Life

Who will cut down
the living greening tree
thoughtlessly?
Our actions speak our soul.
Our soul makes choices.

The Celebration Tree

A glinting flock of goldfinch
brought brightly here
by a warm April wind
chose to decorate the birch tree
like a Christmas tree
weighting down its branches in smooth arcs
as they pecked diligently at it.

Bugs or buds
what does it matter they were after?
They were golden and gray-gold baubles
hanging head-down, gobbling
making a Resurrection Christmas tree
out of a birch tree.

Cover The Earth
With Love

Great Dispenser
give us love to spread abroad.
Shake us with your breath
like the wind
shakes the apple blossoms
making them spread their whiteness
over the eager ground.

He Was Man

Lord, did you love your land as I love mine?
As you wandered on the hills of Galilee
and viewed the loveliness of flower and tree
did your heart beat high because that land was thine?
And on the lake, oh, Lord, was ever lake like thine
without compare, blue on the golden days
like our dear river is, or turning lacy grays
with rain and mist? And was your heart like mine
to see the new green shoots come in the spring
to marvel at the way God made them grow
to know the spring sun, feel the fresh wind blow
and hear the magic when a bird did sing?

And when the time drew near for you to go
and your shattered body hung upon the cross
did you shudder human-like for the deep loss
of hills, and lake, and fields, and air, although
you knew that you would walk abroad again
when Easter dawn came on Jerusalem?

As We Edge Further Into May and The Dogwood Petals Ripple to the Ground

May is the green month
after the flourish and trumpet calls of April.
After the bugle of golden daffodils
the green settles in.

The trees thrust green against the sky
and we are overwhelmed with green.
Thank God for the green God-given earth.
Thank God for infinite acres of green
to rest our eyes, our souls.

Let Me Sing

sunsets and rainy days.
Let me sing May.
Let me sing now.
Give me a voice and words.
Let me stop thinking about it.
Let me sing.

Give me a big heart.
Let me love all the world.
Let me love it now.
Let me stop thinking about it.
Just let me love it--
starting now.

Give me the power to help.
Let me help forever and ever.
Let me help now.
Let me start helping
and not stop.
Let me start now.

To Atlas Holding Up The Earth

The world does not depend completely
on your effort.
You can relax
for a few moments each day
and the world will not fall apart.
For just a few moments each day
trust God.

Let God take charge
and you will see
that God is good
at earth-holding.

How Each Tree Shouts
"Glory To God"
in Its Own Way

When I behold in every tree
a dreadful similarity
and catch, in glancing at one face
the pattern of the human race
to live and then to die
then I must prod me to recall
that one who was the best of all
took on our frame
shouldered our shame
and died to show us
death is not the end
of bodies that have souls
and he did send
his spirit sweeping out
a victory tide
of new and shining life
to our awaiting forms.

On The Shore of The Great Sea

I like to feel the sand
running through my hand
sands of time
running through my hand.

I like to feel the air
as it whispers in my hair
wind of time
whispering eternity.

Summertime

Energy

Early morning
is a tiger about to pounce
on her prey knowing the pride
of a meat find for little ones
every muscle alert
claws firm on her perch.

Evening
is the same tiger
chances missed, paws worn
knowing the kittens are hungry.

Will jungle sleep heal all this?

Bird Watching

Envious, earthbound, drab
I have eyed the gulls gliding
dipping for fish, swearing fiercely.
Yes, I could match their swaggering pace
but wings were denied me.

Jealous, shallow, jaded
I have watched the ducks winging
seeming masters of the sky.
How I yearned to buzz heaven with them
until the fiendish bullet struck one.

My Home

There was a home I had.
Oh, how I loved it!
The tall oaks guarded it
and the grass was green
and best of all
my friends were there.
Though we spoke not of it
we had this thought at heart--
we worship here one God
the same God who is love
and for this reason
we are kind, one to another.

Oh, I had a home--
it was too good to last.

When I had trouble
there was always a hand or two
put out to aid me.
In days of joy
how we would share our bounty
flowers and fruits
and greetings of the seasons.

In days of sorrow, loving hearts
helped speed the sadness.

Even the birds knew there
that God was with us.
The chickadees frolicked like children
by the seed we scattered.
The tufted tit-mice looked
like monks strolling together.
I could almost hear them
saying soft rosaries
pacing under the oak trees.

The robin who came in spring
reminded us in joy
of the resurrection of the world
of God saying
"I shall make all things new."

But one night I dreamed a dream
where I left my home
for a land of beauty
and in the land of beauty
I was sorrowful.

When I awoke, I cried
as I looked at the birds
and the green grass and the oaks
"I will never leave you!
How silly can a dream be?"

But today I am in a land of beauty--
sorrowful.

No Place To Hide

Time was when I could hide
my heart from prying eyes.
I could run home
to the warm clover on the hill
to cry my heart out
to be comforted
by the sun and the wind
and the sweet grasses.

Where can I run today?
Back to the old dreams?
They are all bruised
and broken and buried.
Back to the protecting arms
when I know now
how much they needed protection?
Back to the spring on the hillside?
They have ploughed the whole hill
and backed the spring into a swamp.

Must I stand here before you and weep
with no place to hide my humanity?

Memories

The memories pound and roll
on the edge of my mind
like the whipping and whispering waves
wash up on the shell strewn shore of the sea.
They lie in the sun
on the sandy shore of my mind
and God bakes them
and basks them
and lets them return
back to me.

On Harps

*I would be like a poplar tree
strong and straight and supple
and pour out my music
as the winds of life sweep through me.*

A Piece of God's Handiwork

*God is above us and beyond us
yet somehow God is in us!*

*Imagine that! The power
and the glory and the splendor
somehow in us!*

*We are a vital part of all
that makes the world run.
We have a secret thing deep in
that lets us contact God
a spot God formed in us
to keep an open line with love.
That means the little soul in me
so tiny, precious, delicate
can tune in to the knowledge
of all that's great in God.*

*God didn't make this wonder-part
to thrive and then decay.
It's meant to know God's love--
to ponder and perceive
and to somehow fit intricately
into God's being.*

The Hummingbird

God knows our every thought!
(What, do you doubt it?)
Not only knows it, but attends on it!
I do not know how God can be with me
and be with you
and be with everyone of humankind
so personally.
I do not know how this may be.
I only know it's so.

I have a pink Wegelia bush.
Oh, it's a beauty.
It's arms are flung wide open
with its heavy blooms.
It gathers the bees to its flowery bosom
like a welcoming mother.

I admired it Tuesday in the sun
and thought a little thought
a little quiet thought
so small that almost
I forgot I thought it.

I thought, "Oh, God, these bumble bees are nice
but if you really wished to please me
you'd send a hummingbird."

I thought it and forgot it.
There are no hummingbirds around.
The cats have frightened all the birds away
except some wary, hardy little sparrows.

Thursday again I sat near my Wegelia
and then the hummingbird!
The blueness, quickness, smallness of him!

36   *Seasonings*

I thought, "Oh, God, you really know
what pleases me!"
Then I remembered my poor quiet thought
my Tuesday tiny half-forgotten thought.
God really knows our every thought.
You had better believe it.
I'm half afraid to think now.

My Rockettes

See my Rockettes.
They are that line of poplar trees
and all of them move together
so gracefully
at the touch of the wind
that you don't notice one particular tree
but it's the whole mass of trees
dancing together
that sets your heart dancing--
fifty trees moving together--
it's a sight to set your heart dancing.

The Pot God Made

God, why did you
make the earth, the tree?
Why make the robin
or the rose, or me?
Why, oh, why
did you make me?

God answered me
so lovingly
"I made you
to know ecstasy.
On my potter's wheel
I made a form
to know and feel
a form that I could fill
with holy knowing
holy feeling, holy growing--
with myself."

We are jars filled with water
filled with humanness.
God's will has made us wine
wine fit for serving
to the bridegroom
and the beloved guests.
We are like common bread
in the hands of the Great Priest
waiting for the words
"This is my body!"
so that we may go forth
and be Christ.
Be Christs, my comrades!
Let us be Christs.
Spirit of God, proclaim the words
that transform us into Christs.

Joe's Day

Where have you been today, young Joe? Your shirt
has three new rents and is wretched with dirt!
You have scratches all over your legs and arms
enough to give me all sorts of alarms.

Where have you been today, young Joe? Your grin
has berry juice stain right down to your chin
and on your face such a look of content
I can tell that you feel your day well spent.

Where have you been today, young Joe? Your eyes
speak of daisy fields and glorious skies.
You seem ages away from the sad time when
men will give you a gun and say, "Hunt men."
Don't hear them, Joe. They've forgotten the thrill
of how raspberries taste on a summertime hill.

The Bouquet

Today
these zinneas decay
pink, red
sunshine caught in a vase.
Drink in their beauty
for they rot away
today.

There's nothing new.

Heaven's the same.
Grab heaven.
It may flee away
today.

Hand Blown Glass

Our creator has made us
of fine bubble glass
and set us for display
on shelves in the shop window.

Light plays upon us
shines through us
and the glass blower
finds us beautiful
because he has made us.

Oh, it is a shame to see us
later after we are sold!
What uses we are put to!
Our handles are broken off.
We are smashed to smithereens
in carelessness or anger.
We hide in dusty corners
hoping to escape notice.

God, The Tree, and I

I can be aware of you, oh, tree
but can you be aware of me?

God made you for me to see.
Why, oh, God, did you make me?
Did you make me to see this tree
that thinking of the why of tree and me
I might think ultimately of thee?

Did you make me to think of thee?

In A Rainbow

What is it like
to be within a rainbow?

I saw your house
upon a distant hill.
The rainbow sprang
skyward from there.
Surely, your rooms
were bathed with radiance;
you walked on jeweled mist;
your very soul
must have sparkled
vibrated
resonated
with colored light.

Tell me the joy
that must have flowed
from this, your experience
of God's creativity.

The Flute Song

The flute song rings clear in my ears
like a steep mountain waterfall
dropping over deep rocks and shadow
into clear stream and moonlight.
And now it dances like a ballerina--
first on one light toe and then
whirling and tripping to the other.
How precise and gay it is!

Woman

God said: I will make woman in my image
cover the earth with her
give her the tools for keeping peace
creating life, building with love.

God said: Let her be mistress
of the birds, the fish, the beasts
that roam the garden I have made.

God blessed the woman, saying:
Go-- and be fulfilled
in serving and creating
as myself.

A Statement Open for Discussion

There is one thing that the creator
of heaven and earth cannot do
that people can do--
that is, to make love visible to people.

For this reason God had to create people.
If there were no people
to love and be loved
love would not exist
and God could not exist.

Come, Sing With Me

I put my heart to music
and the tune went like this--
a hand clasp, some laughter
and a long, sweet kiss.

I put my soul to music
and the song seemed dread.
It went, "Suffer for the sinner,"
and "Pray for the dead."

The heart's music floated off
like ashes on the sea
but the soul's music swelled with love
that filled eternity.

Think of What Is Most Beautiful

This being is more beautiful than sunrise
more beautiful than the crescent moon
holding a star in her arms
more exquisite than a flower
more perfect than a snow crystal
more majestic than mountain peaks
shimmering in moonlight
more gentle than the kindest deed
that you have ever done
for one you love.

How can a being be so beautiful?

***I Am** is too much for our vision to absorb.*

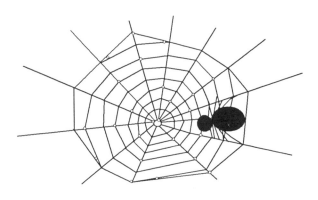

How Spiders Trapped The Sun

The spiders were roaming the world that night
blowing, rolling out of sight
crawling in crevices, dim and obscure.
They found them a corner of musty kegs
and they danced there on jointed, clicking legs.

The webs formed there like sparkling glass
brittle and crystal in the night
reflecting the light that hurtled past
fairy things of moonbeam gleam
made by waving, weaving, spinning tight.

This piece to this, that piece to that
each strand woven neat and pat
each strand depending on one before
each strand expending one strand more
so comes the dawn, what a glittering sight!

They have trapped them jewels of dew
and in each droplet cupped a piece of sun!
What profit for a night so dark begun!
True life is purchased with such priceless coin.
God helps our flimsey deeds to catch the sunrise.

On The Overgrown Grave
of John Desmond

This is a living cemetery--
look, John Desmond, how that
small oak climbs between
your headstone
and your footstone, like it had sprung
straight from your navel.

It is hard not to think
that your eyes are someplace
up in that oak tree
watching me
for, after all, the oak tree is made
from the stuff of your body.

What does it say
here on your head stone?
"Death is a debt to nature due
which I have paid and so must you."
I feel no qualms about
tramping on your grave.
Why, the whole woods here
is full of you.

Each Has Her Own Gold

I had a bird in a golden cage--
a golden bird-- orange and gold.
I kept him there for many an age.
Ah, he was lovely to behold.

Have you heard-- I forgot the little gold bird?

His song was golden like his down
the most cheerful song I've ever heard.
All he asked for his tumult of joy
was seed and water and a soft, kind word.

What a deed!-- I forgot his water and seed!

I got so used to his musical cheers
telling the world of his delight
I forgot to feed him for months, for years
and now he is such a pitiful sight.

Don't say, "Shame!" You might do the same.

Chesapeake Bay Pier

There are fish that swim
in and out
sunlight and shadow
under the pier, child so dear.
There are two blue swallows
flashing in and out
dark and light
midnight blue when the moon is shining
horizon gold when the sun is setting
flashing their wings
in and out
sunlight and shadow
under the pier, child so dear
in and out
under the pier.
There are bugs that crawl
around on the planks
of the pier, child so dear
bugs for the two flashing birds
and down below
where the cool salt water
curls and laps
under the water
and under the pier
are so many wonderful things
clinging shells and floating weeds
and things too small
to see at all
with our eyes
little child so dear
in this private world
of under the pier.
God has made it all
so wonderful here
under the pier.

Why Am I?

Back to the roots, to the fundamentals
to the original seed, to the eternal questions
the "Why am I here?, Who am I?
Who sent me?" But in me
only deep in myself
are the answers to what I ask myself.

Who put me here to praise what caused it all?
Who takes me by the hand to show me
the vastness of these works past comprehension?
Who invites me gently to see
the earth whirling around the sun
the sun doing its fast dance
on the outskirts of the Milky Way Galaxy
which is but a minor field of stars spinning
amongst a cosmos of galaxies all rushing off
at unbelievable paces from each other.
Rushing endlessly? Perhaps--
I do not know--
too far for me to comprehend or care.

Who put me here to see all this
to stretch my sight beyond its seeing?
Who put me here to praise?
My heart has answers.

I know that Someone made me, knows me.
Someone made this big immenseness
this enormity that urges to create forms of life
to praise what caused it.

In me there is the achievement, the fulfillment
a creature who can see God's creation
and say, "I believe."

Be Merry!

Are we repeating
what villians and vipers
are voicing
instead of rejoicing?

The Cardinal

Bless the little bird I watch
and bless his song.
His song is praise
to that which made him.
His song is prayer.

The very rocks praise God
simply by being
but rocks have never sung
so wise a prayer
as this that is all joy.

Prayer is a love song
to the Lord, and, oh
so full a lovesong comes
from this small throat.

The music soars gently to heaven.
May my soul ride beside it
soaring up to find its God
with this wild prayer
for sweet companion.

Our World

God made this!
Feel it.
See it.
Smell it.

Crumble it in your fingers.
Send rumpled rips of greening leaves
tumbling downwards
and think of atoms joining atoms
of cells, of glucose
of inward scientific workings
beyond our human capabilities.

Hold the grass shoots humbly
and admire them.
God made them
and we can only wonder
at such handiwork
and worship.

The Cycle

As the sun draws vapor
from the ocean
which then rains down
upon the earth
so does God draw
good thoughts, good deeds
sweet prayers from us
melding them
in heavenly places
to a cloud of holy spirit
that is then poured out on us.

Cedar Hill

Nothing changes here.
The trees stay the same
big, hanging.
The birds chatter
and the cicadas are still singing.

The tombstones don't change
solid granite, they will do
for my lifetime.

And Mom does not change.
I can still see her
walking across the open field
in her white dress
still bouncing along
at over ninety
still hear her German-touched English
exclaiming, "Today you go forth
to bring life and health
and love
to all you meet!"

Each time I come here
she tells me the same thing.
Nothing changes here.

Our Freedom To Be

If there were no death
what would we make of life?

Shouting

The ocean spues her mighty spray
against the land whereon I stand
troubled in heart, but eager yet to sing
the message of the king
(the king who is the Rock where I retire).

Yes, the very waves wash up
and shift the sands beneath my feet
and throw their dew upon my face and hair
and chill my cheek
(the waves that are the tumult of desire).

Trembling I stand
a young Demosthenes upon the shore
hurtling my garbled wind-swept words
against the billows' roar.
(Oh, that my speech were silver tried in fire!)

God Audible

The heavens declare the glory of God--
in majestic silence
proclaim a loving creator--
but in humankind
God becomes audible.
Imagine--
we can articulate God!

Wasted Glory

Look at you, white lily
on your last bloom
of an amazing crown
of six white goblets!

I would have come by
but it was too hot
to leave the house
but how could I
have ignored you so?
Couldn't I at least
have run out for a moment
to say, "Good morning.
How's your health?"

You were doing your best
to praise God
and I passed you by.
What a waste of the stupendous!

I only saw you
when taking out the garbage.

Wiser

As I grow older
I love the flowers more.
I understand how hard it is
for them to grow.

The Good Returns To God

The urge to good and its opposite
are rooted together in us
and can't be separated.

We question all our lives
what road is optimum.

Death comes to everyone
and what is profitable
goes back to God.

Why Flowers Grow

God made the flowers grow to cheer mankind
because God loves us. Thus God planned it so
before the world began. God wills we know
their beauty. Let me ask, "Why do you find
such colors, shapes, and forms?" I say that shows
a thoughtful overseer. God made the flowers
to cheer sad hearts, and gladden gladsome hours.
Why, everywhere man goes, some flower grows!

How can you still persist it was by chance?
Dear unbelieving friend, arouse and see
the glories here surrounding you and me.
There could have been no lovelier mischance.

If this is chance, why then I must lament--
the world is space's best planned accident.

Transformation of Energy

It takes the human being
to transform God's energy
into good deeds.

In the same manner
a waterfall employs generators
to transform its power
into something usable.

Mocking Thoughts

The mockingbird is singing in the dry afternoon.
I know what he is saying.
He is a troublemaker from away back
but he tells the truth.
His notes are sharp and bitter on my ear.

The mockingbird sings to the full moon at midnight.
I waken to hear him
and there is no place to hide
when God comes walking into my soul
when the truth lies out in the open.

What does my soul look like?
Is it sharp and clean like a mockingbird's whistle?
Is it full of deep black holes like the heavens
where the black is so weighty it draws things to it
and pulls all the light rays in after it
like a closed door?

God Watches

The clouds come.
The clouds go
sunlight and shadow over the earth.
God watches.
God is good. I have seen God
stroking the silk-eared corn in wonder and admiration.
What a strange thing, corn
but from it sprang the beginnings of civilization
that man might know God
better, sooner.
God is good.
I have seen God
placing the long-tailed comets
high out among the stars
and smiling.
"Thus will men know me better.
Thus will they glean more knowledge
of me and my creation.
Thus they will come closer to truth and to wisdom
sooner, sooner."
God is good.
I have seen God
yearning, yearning
to have us turn to wisdom
sooner, sooner
that all our moaning, groaning in creation
might be swallowed into the mouth of gold eternity
sooner, sooner
for our sakes only
who know times and boundaries.
(Not for God's sake
for God knows all things
in their completion and conception.)
God watches.
God loves us before forever.

Autumn

Monarch Butterflies

Long ago
before there were small boys
to run in autumn fields
God thought
"I will make milkweed pods
for little boys
to take apart and scatter
on the autumn winds."
God thought
"I will make butterflies to feed
on this strange weed
so that small boys can be caught breathless
seeing orange wings rising against blue sky."

The Butterfly

Who made the butterfly?
What fancy whim put flower on the wing?
Who made the butterfly?
Who, but God
a loving, happy God.

And who made man
this creature of caprice
of evil and of good?
Who, but God
a loving, happy God.

How my heart ached
when I found flower-on-the-wing
caught in a spider's web
and sister spider sitting there
horrified at what big game she'd taken
marveling at how easily
she had taken it.

Likewise, advertisers and other plotters
must be amazed
at how easily we fall into entrapments
sometimes as if we were eager to plunge in!

How carefully I freed flower-on-the-wing.
How carefully I pulled the web
from fragile feet and wings
with bits of leaf and stick.
But such a shock he'd had
he could not fly away.

May we not fall into the snares of irresponsibility.
Though God deliver us so gently
it may be hard to use our wings again.

French Alps

I have fallen in love with the mountains.
Today they are covered with snow
and there's shadings of light and darkness
as the rainclouds come and go.

The tallest is called Argenterra
and the other night, what do you think--
The rosy hued clouds of the sunset
had covered her over with pink.

But they are brave young mountains!
When the wind-swept sea waves roar
proud and clear against the sky
they march fiercely down to the shore.

On Change

All things change.
We cannot hold them here within our hand.
The daisy in the grass
is beautiful today; tomorrow, gone.
Today's sad tear becomes tomorrow's smile.
The smile will pass from lip to lip
and turn to a good deed.
The bit of leaven acts upon the bread.
The mustard comes from but a tiny seed.
To deep eternity a word Christ said
dwells in the hearts of folk to guide them right.
The candle flickering in the window changes
fear of the dark to joy that lights the night.
The small things turn to big as God arranges
and opposites surprise us--
peace from strife.
Calm comes from out of storm.
Death turns to life.

Funeral Bells--Cagnes Sur Mer

We heard the church bells chiming

"DEAD!
    DEAD!
        DEAD!
            RIS'N!"

there by the sparkling azure sea
with their sonorous, telling timing

"EARTH!
    EARTH!
        EARTH!
            HEAV'N!"

That souls from bodies should be free
seemed suddenly to us so right.

"PAIN!
    PAIN!
        PAIN!
            JOY!"

Now, only joy; no need for sighing
here on the beach in bright sunlight with

"DONG!
    DONG!
        DONG!
            DING!"

the fishermen's quiet talk, and the gulls' crying.

The Penalty

Long ago
when I still plucked roses
to pin in my hair
I woke in the night
knowing
the sentence of death
was upon me.

Since then
many times I have roused up
to meet the black emptiness
so now I am friends
with the thought.
It no longer churns
my insides.

Last night
I suddenly realized
we all have to die
the great, the wild
the old, the young
my friends
the bad, the good
the earth.
So much riot and movement
turned into
stillness and element.

It is the stillness
that is so frightening.

Eternal rest!
How can death make us rest
who can't sit still a minute!

In The Forest

I have caught glimpses of him
as I battled my way through the forest.
The forest is dark and cold
and thick and gloomy
and there is no one to tell me the way.

I have caught glimpses of him
and then I did not think
"Why am I here in this forest?"
or "Why am I separate from him?"
or "What is the way through the wood?"

I have caught glimpses of him
as I battled my way through the bushes
as I stomped the thorns underfoot
and the branches snapped back in my face
and my arms were scratched and bleeding.

I have caught glimpses of him
and then-- the forest was a garden
and I did not think of anything
but "How beautiful he is!
How beautiful he is!"

Obedient,

I reached to drink the golden cup. He said
"You have no need to drink. I drank for you."
Can he be dead!

They Died That I Might Live

I would go back to the autumn hill
and listen
for the sound of their voices
in the wind that stirs the trees
and that shakes the droplets of dew
that glimmer and glisten
as the sunrise fingers
the trembling golden leaves.

What did they say?
What were the truths they told me?
I need to remember them now
as never before
when these barbed wire shackles
that ever so firmly hold me
cut into my flesh and rankle
and chafe me sore.

I would go back
to the edge of my beginning
when time was simple
and love was love
and peace was peace
when murder was kill, was wrong
and had to be punished
when those who ruled us
had made all wars to cease
when men gave their lives
for a truth that others thundered.

Was it worth dying for?
I have often wondered.

Old Barns

Some of us have barns in our childhood
color of dusk-deep red-brown velvet
accented with rusted gutters and hinges
barns of big beams
of largeness, of strength
secure walls
holding the world together.

Some of us have rested
comfortable, content, loved
on a hay bale, and watched light
filtering through hay dust
like truth penetrating populations.

Some of us have listened in the darkness
to the scritch of scurrying mice
and discovered priorities in humility.
Some have brushed against
the meditative webs of spiders
and absorbed their wisdom and patience.

Some of us have thoughts
that still dwell inside secure vastness
have minds that know
inside the darkness
there is life.

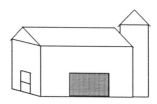

Evening

Gray shadows of night settling in
but we have a fire here
and hearts that laugh together.
We can look forward to the sparkling stars
gaze upward without fear
in autumn's wind blown weather.

Indian Summer

This is the song of a golden September
a song of tall sun-flowers and deep purple asters
a song of warm sun and clear air.
This is the song of a month to remember
when burnt logs on cool nights fall ember from ember
and the day is like glorious prayer.

This is the month when the full moon's bright yellow.
Our night turns to day in the face of its radiance
and fields are enticing and gay.
This month the night sky is velvet and mellow
the heart is at one with the heart of one's fellow
and love turns the world on its way.

Looking Towards Harvest

When we die, and willingly return
to that great force
that drew us on this sea
perhaps a living, sparkling yield of energy
will stack in stalks at harvest time
will gleam and glow
and flash among the stars
will flow where great tides flow
yet who can know?

Sensing Forces

Rain in September
and white swans gathering
on the black water--
gathering together
knowing
they're going--
together.

We gather, too
on the wet fall
gold-leafed days
not knowing
what winter will bring--
wanting to feel
the being of each other--
sensing that together
we might amount to
a force to be reckoned with
against whatever forces
might disturb the surface
of the black water
under the gold-leafed trees.

Fall Waltz

This is the waltz of the fall
the dignified dance
of golden oak
of reddening dogwood
of all the trees, so stately in the sun.

Oh, Lord, it's fall!
May I dance, too?
Yes, stately me
an old-gold oak
riotous with color
catching eyes
and pointing up to heaven.

Let all folk see
that God made me
made fall
made age
made world
made heaven
and it's all glorious.
It's glorious.

We dancers run the gamut
from pale beech
to purple sumach.
Just see us
swinging out our waltz.
Just look at us
and think of God!

Leaves, Pebbles, and People

Have you searched through the October leaves
hoping to find the just right one, the perfect one
and as you picked each one
cast it aside for another
for each had its imperfection?
Leaves look better in bunches.
Leaves look glorious in October
rioting together across the landscape.

Have you searched the pebbles on the beach
for the just right pebble
the one to take home to varnish
and to use for a paper weight?
Have you cast aside one after another
for they were all imperfect?

Have you searched among people
hoping to find the perfect friend
the one to bear your burdens
your confidences, your imperfections?
Have you found anyone
good enough to love you
and to fill in your lacks?

People do better in groups
where the gifts of some
shade out the others' deficiencies.

Loving humanity in community
is worth searching for
and can be found
by the loving and persistent.

Who Hears The Owl?

The owl sings at night
vibrant, bone-chilling
across the distances.
What good is
a loud clear voice in the night?
Who hears it?
The jays are dreaming their dreams.
The goldfinch is sleeping.
Nobody listens.
Nobody cares.

The owl has joy to tell
across a hollow world
filling the silence
thrilling empty hearts.
Willing he is to listen.
Willing he is to share
trilling through the vast reaches
"Is there anyone out there?"

Swans

Three swans on the water
saying something about trinity
swans in October sunlight.
Suddenly
there is a flurry of white wings
too many to count
descending, joining
intermingling
saying something about community
about spirit and holiness
about wholeness
about souls
ready to do justice and mercy.

The Month of Remembering

The waste between here and the quarry
is a tumble-down, a melee
of blown trees and bent red shumach
curtseying to this mad October wind
and over to one side the field sun flowers
spring up and down in wild exhilaration.

Down in that dip that travels to the pond
the low weeds rustle 'round in ecstasy
feeling a cold wet kiss on dying leaves
yet frightened, knowing it to be the last.

Rash October, month I love because of sorrow
month I love because of sweet things dying beautifully
month I love because of wildness
sudden rages, and sweet calms
month of hard rains and rattling winds
and month of Indian summer
month of warm leaf-fire fragrance
old October-- month of realization
life-blood month of the year--

let me hear your rash winds echo
down the streets of my mind forever
let me feel your cold wet kiss in my heart;
let me remember your leaves falling;
let me remember your warm days
and far away nights
when sparks flew to the treetops
from autumn fires.

Let me become a part of you, October
let me be knit
into the innermost parts
of your violent days.

October

Sing? I shall sing of turning shades on trees
of browning oaks, and maples' arch gold mines.
I'll melodize the sumach's purple leaves
and shout with joy at reddish ivy vines.

Yes, I shall gasp delighted at the fashion
of a single golden-rod that's turning gray
and clutch into my hands and crush with passion
one small lone aster fading to decay.

I shall clasp my hands with depthless bliss
smelling the smoke of leafy autumn fires
and shiver at the thrill of one sweet kiss
from this warm autumn wind fraught with desires.

Sing? I shall sing as if this heart would cry
when sudden o'er a hill I cross and see
a thousand tones of red against the sky--
a heaven-painted frosted beechnut tree.

Sing? I shall sing like you were here today
beside me, walking, kicking up the leaves
and throwing handfuls in my face in play
and loving me, and loving all the trees

and loving all the graying autumn flowers
and drinking in deep draughts of ecstasy.
I'll sing for there'll be other autumn hours
after God has brought you back again to me.

Elegy To The Locust Tree

The shreiking saw has left its mark
on fifty feet of towering bark
and you lie crumbling in the dark.
I taste a mouth full of regret
to see your sunken silhouette.
Death waits us all, we can't forget.

Yes, you were young when I was young.
On you, spring's gay white flowers have hung.
By you, the wren and thrush have sung.

For you, too, came one terrible night
when the unpredictable streak of light
came from the sky with power to smite
but you stood firm and you have shown
that great hearts have no need to moan
though fate may split them to the bone.

Now, crawling age ate past repair
before we caught its ugly stare.
We could not leave you rotting there.
So you must rest and I must rest
and who can say it is not best
to sleep thus gently with the blest?

But still I cannot call you dead
for trees like you I've heard it said
when they are felled send up new head
and where the living writhing root
comes near the air, may institute
a possibly tenacious shoot.

So, too, do good ideas regain
from seeming loss and bitter pain
a new foothold on the terrain.

Thank You For Earth and Time

Gold and silver
the willows and maples claim November.
They clamour, "Eucharistio."
Gold and silver early winter dreams
of the Messiah coming
possibilities of love and wisdom
filling a material earth.
Love **can** *be placed*
in a gold and silver vessel
when that container
is an earth made by
a gracious God.

Hudson Cliffs

Three hundred years ago
the eagle clung here
and raucoused his call
across November.

The water sparkled
as it does today
like myriad diamonds
as the wind ruffles it
as the sun pierces the wave peaks
from its low angle in the south.

Three hundred years ago
beneath the sparkle
there were flashes of silver
and trout colored like rainbows.

Today we have new words--
PCBs, kepone
words that do not sparkle
words that sink to the bottom
and settle with silt.

All Saints' Day

Saint Therese

I am a light house
by the sea
sending
my steady beam of light
far off
so those tossed
on the waves of night
may find the shore
through me.

I am a light!
Then, too
I am a bell!
Swinging aloft
in my strong tower
I say to all
that now
is time to pray
and time to live
their small lives
well.

So I am sound!
Also, I am a flower
a little flower
that crushed by chance
under the coarse foot
of circumstance
spreads lovely perfume
through the hour.

You Can't Keep Saints From Marching

They have turned the earth to love
to kind and caring love!
They have turned their hands to lift
the loads from others backs.
They have fed the hungry world
with food from their own fields.
We can do likewise! Let us do!
There's need for us imperfect folk
to cheer each other on.

The Name of God

Your name is Being

Being--
in the bright planets
that cluster in the morning sky--

Being--
in the shadow of sunrise
that rests on the western hill--

Being--
in the flock of birds
that pause from migration
in the leafless trees--

Being--
in a friend's heart
that shares joy
and shares sorrow.

Oh, Lord, my God
how beautiful is your name
in all the earth!

Advent

The "O" Antiphons

O Wisdom, Word of God, Giver of Care so tender
answer your people's prayer, O Merciful Mender.
Of true salvation be the swift sender.

O Sacred One of Israel, Giver of Law, Presence of Being
Come, dwell in our hearts, All-knowing, All-seeing.
For those imprisoned, be the All-freeing.

O Flower of Jesse's Stem, Child of a Humble Maid
of you all peoples, tyrants, popes are sore afraid
for you come strongly to our aid.

O Key of David, all gates open to your key.
Hell, death, and heaven know full well your royalty
and stand aside as you set captives free.

O Radiant Dawn, The Splendor of New Light
O Sun of Justice, keep us in your sight.
Shine through the darkness of our night!

O King of Nations, Joy of Every Soul
though we are dust, instill the heavenly goal
in every spirit, making all things whole.

Go with the nations of the world, O Emmanuel
Savior of Peoples, Blessed Desire of All
help us together, that we may not fall.

His Name

Herod:
> *You say you have found him.*
> *What is his name?*
> *Tell me, that I may worship him also.*
> *Tell me, that I may proclaim his fame.*

Melchior:
> *His name is King, the Anointed One*
> *Prince of Peace, Bright Star of Morning*
> *Lord of the Heavens, Prince of All Peoples*
> *Off Shoot of Jesse, Scion of David.*
> *His name is Leader, Light.*
> *His name is Way.*

Caspar:
> *His name is Deity, Eternal Father*
> *Mighty God, Wisdom, Spirit of Yahweh*
> *Spirit of Power, Spirit of Knowledge*
> *Spirit of Counsel.*
> *His name is Truth.*

Balthasar:
> *His name is Adam. He is Man*
> *Man of Sorrows, Seeker and Cornerstone*
> *Servant and Shepherd.*
> *His name is Savior.*
> *His name is Sacrifice*
> *Lamb, Love Eternal.*
> *His name is Life.*

Christmas
at
Women's Correctional Facility

Christmas makes you
long for a home
ridden of roaches
where the lesbian
down the corridor
can't hang onto you
in her loneliness
and frustration;
where you can
digest a meal
or a good thought
instead of having
life thrown at you
like a closed fist.

But faith, hope, love
can dwell here
gifts from
the Great Giver.
Alma knows that
the Jews got out of Egypt
that the Just Judge
will get us home
one of these holidays.

Winnie comforts us
by telling us
that the baby Jesus
wasn't at home either
that first Christmas.

Taking Down The Christmas Tree

The tree
says to me
"Ouch!
What are you doing?
Here I have been standing
radiant
in your life
like a bride
bedecked
with jewels
a sign of peace
in strife
a glow
that draws all eyes.
And you cut me!
Strike me!
Snatch my wealth!"

Oh, how I hate to take the tree down!

Christ stands in the living room of my heart.
He says to me
"Ouch!
What are you doing?"

Over The River

On this cold winter's day
just past that sassafras that is so twisted
from having the grapevine
clung and hung all over it
just over the evergreens
the cedar, pine, and spruce
just past that sturdy oak tree
I catch a glimpse of the beautiful
a glimpse of grandeur
a glimpse of what the psalmist
called "the everlasting."
These are the hills, the Catskills
a wee bit bluer than the blue sky of this day
just that much deeper in color
that I know they are there.

So, too, just past the cares of this world
the house cleaning, the cooking
the caring for the children
our duties to others, our worries
our thoughts and our aspirations
why, I catch a small glimpse of Thee
the Eternal, the Everlasting
just enough to know that you are there.

Someday I shall trudge through the woods
and pass over the river that flows between
and climb the foothills and be close
to the mountains in all their glory.

Someday I shall go
beyond the cares of this world
and pass over the river.

The Failure

Once upon a time
in a faraway land
I had a dream.
I was young and lovely
and the whole world loved me.
They knelt around my feet
and spoke praise
even before I had done anything
to be praised
and I knew
that I would do
great things.

The world was young
and it was springtime.
I put in my plants and watered them well.
They grew and flourished.

Summer came
and summer was wonderful.
The world was wonderful
but someplace along the way
there was a drought
and some of my seedlings dried up.
Though I saw
and hastened to care for the rest
the summer turned out to be a cruel one.
I had to stand there
and watch my plantings wither and die.

There was no place to go for water.

It slowly came to me
that this was my life
that there would be
no other spring
no more planting time.

Fall was here
and I had nothing to show for it
but a handful of last year's seed
no harvest
no lush fruits
only a handful of last year's seed
and no new springs to plant it.

Winter is coming!
God of Existence
I beg for mercy.
What shall I do?
The summer was a hard one.

Let me take my small handful of seed
and give it to someone
who will have a spring and summer yet to come.

I shall give it to someone and say
"The seed is good.
It will yield a hundred fold.
It was the summer that did it in."

I shall warn them
to be sure to have a store of water.

The Clothes
We Wear
on
our
Soul

A brittle china case
covers our soul
a feeble tent
that falls into decay.
We carry it around
and cling to it
not knowing
what great God
it keeps from us.

Eternity

Built stones
men's bones
green grass
all pass.

Stars fade
black shade
horn blows.

Soul knows
Thy word
still heard.